Eucharist

NIHIL OBSTAT
Rev. Msgr. Glenn D. Gardner, J.C.D.
Censor Librorum

IMPRIMATUR
† Most Rev. Charles V. Grahmann
Bishop of Dallas

May 27, 2002

The Nihil Obstat and Imprimatur are official declarations that the material reviewed is free of doctrinal or moral error. No implication is contained therein that those granting the Nihil Obstat and Imprimatur agree with the contents, opinions, or statements expressed.

Send all inquiries to:
RCL • Resources for Christian Living
200 East Bethany Drive
Allen, Texas 75002-3804

Toll Free   877-275-4725
Fax   800-688-8356

Visit us at www.FaithFirst.com

Printed in the United States of America
by ColorDynamics, Allen, Texas

20441   ISBN 0-7829-1005-X (Child's Book)
20442   ISBN 0-7829-1006-8 (Guide)

5 6 7 8 9 10 11 12
07 08 09 10 11 12

ACKNOWLEDGMENTS

Excerpts from the English translation of *Rite of Baptism for Children* © 1969, International Committee on English in the Liturgy, Inc. (ICEL); excerpts from the English translation of *The Roman Missal* © 1973, International Committee on English in the Liturgy (ICEL); excerpts from the English translation of *Rite of Confirmation, 2nd Edition* © 1975, International Committee on English in the Liturgy, Inc. All rights reserved.

PHOTO CREDITS

Abbreviated as follows: (bkgd) background; (t) top; (b) bottom; (l) left; (r) right; (c) center.

Chapter 1: Page 4 (l), © David Young-Wolff/Photo Edit; 4 (r), © Michael Newman/Photo Edit; 5, © Jeff Rotman/The Image Bank; 8-9, © Bill & Peggy Wittman; 10, © The Crosiers/Gene Plaisted,OSC; 11, © The Crosiers/Gene Plaisted,OSC.

Chapter 2: Page 14 (l), © FPG International; 14 (r), © Banana Stock, Ltd/PictureQuest; 15 © Mary Kate Denny/Photo Edit; 18, © Eric Williams/RCL; 19, © The Crosiers/Gene Plaisted, OCS.

Chapter 3: Page 22 (l), © Paul Merideth/Stone; 22 (r), © Jilly Wendell/Stone; 23 © Ron Chapple/ThinkStock/PictureQuest; 26, © The Crosiers/Gene Plaisted, OSC; 27, © Eric Williams/RCL.

Chapter 4: Page 30 (l), © Digital Vision/PictureQuest; 30 (r), © Sandra Stambaugh/Index Stock/PictureQuest; 31 © PhotoDisc; 34, © Eric Williams/RCL; 35, © Eric Williams/RCL.

Chapter 5: Page 38 (l), © The Image Bank; 38 (r), © Myrleen Ferguson Cate/Photo Edit/PictureQuest; 39, © Photographer's Library Ltd./eStock Photography/PictureQuest; 42, © The Crosiers/Gene Plaisted, OSC.; 43,© Eric Williams/RCL.

Chapter 6: Page 46 (l), © Owen Franken/Corbis; 46 (r), © EyeWire; 47, © Chris Cole/The Image Bank; 50, © Eric Williams/RCL; 51, © Eric Williams/RCL.

Chapter 7: Page 54 (l), © John Giustina/FPG International; 54 (r), © Richard Hutchings/Photo Edit/PictureQuest; 55, © David Young-Wolff/Photo Edit/ PictureQuest; 58, © Eric Williams/RCL; 59, © James L. Shaffer; 64, © Eric Williams/RCL.

Backmatter: Page 65, © Eric Williams/RCL; 66, © Eric Williams/RCL; 67, © Eric Williams/RCL; 68 (l), © The Crosiers/Gene Plaisted, OSC; 68 (r), © Eric Williams/RCL; 70 (l), © Eric Williams/RCL; 70 (r), © Eric Williams/RCL; 71, © Eric Williams/RCL; 80, © Tony Jambor.

Illustrations: Jenny Williams/Portfolio Solutions, pp. 6–7, 16–17, 24–25, 32–33, 40–41, 48–49, 56–57.

Cover Design: Kristy O. Howard
Cover Illustration: Karen Malzeke-McDonald

Dedication

**This program is dedicated to
Richard C. Leach
1927–2001
founder and continuing inspiration of RCL
and recipient of the Pro Ecclesia et Pontifice Cross
bestowed by Pope John Paul II in recognition
of outstanding service to the Church.**

SACRAMENT PREPARATION DEVELOPMENT TEAM

Developing a sacrament program requires the talents of many gifted people working together as a team. RCL is proud to acknowledge these dedicated people who contributed to the development of this sacrament preparation program.

Mary Beth Jambor
Writer

**Jacquie Jambor
Diane Lampitt**
Contributing Writers

Rev. Louis J. Cameli
Theological Advisor

Rev. Robert D. Duggan
Liturgical Advisor

Elaine McCarron, SCN
Catechetical Advisor

Marina A. Herrera
Hispanic Consultant

Lisa Brent
Art and Design Director

**Pat Bracken
Kristy O. Howard**
Designers

Laura Fremder
Electronic Page Makeup

Jenna Nelson
Production Director

**Patricia A. Classick
Ronald C. Lamping**
Project Editors

**Joseph Crisalli
Demere Henson**
Web Site Producers

Ed DeStefano
General Editor

Maryann Nead
President/Publisher

Contents

We Belong

Loving God,
thank you for
the gift of Baptism.

Sharing Together

In the opening prayer we blessed ourselves with water. We made the sign of the cross. What was it like for you to bless yourself with water?

How is water part of your life?

As Catholics we often bless ourselves with water and make the sign of the cross. Give one example of a time when you bless yourself with water or make the sign of the cross.

In the church and the chapel

The Baptism of Jesus

In the Bible we read stories about Jesus and water. Read this Bible story. Discover what happened when Jesus came to the Jordan River.

One day Jesus came to the Jordan River. Seeing John the Baptist in the water, Jesus said to him, "Baptize me as you are baptizing the other people."

John said to Jesus, "You do not need to be baptized."

Jesus answered, "For now, do as I ask you."

Jesus walked down into the water, and John baptized him. When Jesus came up out of the water, he saw the Spirit of God like a dove come down upon him. Jesus also heard a voice saying, "You are my Son. I love you."

Based on Matthew 3:13–17

FAITH FOCUS

What happened at the baptism of Jesus?

Jesus was baptized by John. How was your baptism like Jesus' baptism?

TOGETHER AS A FAMILY

Share the Bible story of the baptism of Jesus. For example: Draw a picture of the story. Family members could add different elements to the same picture. Then share responses to the question on this page.

We Belong 7

Our Baptism

WHAT WE SEE AND HEAR

At Baptism we see water, oil, a white garment, and a lighted candle. The oil reminds us that we have been chosen as God's special children. The white garment reminds us that God has given us new life. The lighted candle reminds us that we have received the gift of faith. We bring light to the world when we live our faith.

Just as Jesus was baptized with water, the Church uses water in the sacrament of Baptism. The sacraments are signs of God's love for us. They are celebrations of the Church that Jesus gave to us. Jesus is present with us in the sacraments. The things that we do and the words that we say in a sacrament show that God is sharing his life and love with us.

We become full members of the Church by celebrating three sacraments. These sacraments are called the Sacraments of Initiation. The Sacraments of Initiation are Baptism, Confirmation, and Eucharist.

Water reminds us of life and living things. Baptism gives us new life. Baptism joins us to Jesus and to all the followers of Jesus. We become members of the Church. Our sins are forgiven. We receive the gift of the Holy Spirit. We receive Baptism only one time.

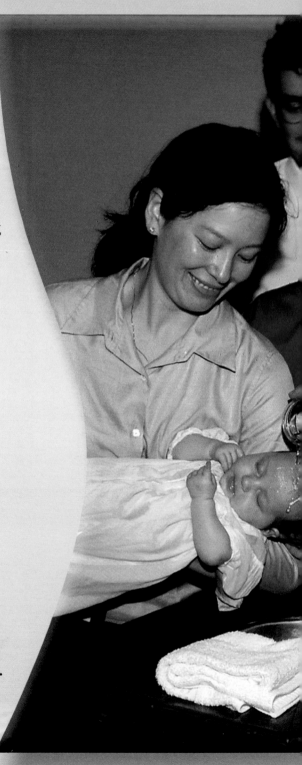

In Baptism the priest or deacon pours water over our head three times, or lowers us into the water three times. As he does this he says, "I baptize you in the name of the Father, and of the Son, and of the Holy Spirit."

Next the priest or deacon rubs blessed oil on the top of our head. We call this anointing. This shows that Baptism marks us as belonging to Jesus forever. We have received the gift of the Holy Spirit.

The Holy Spirit is the third Person of the Holy Trinity. The name *Trinity* tells what God has told us about himself. There is one God in three Persons—God the Father, God the Son, and God the Holy Spirit. The Holy Spirit is always with us. The Holy Spirit teaches us to pray. The Holy Spirit helps us to know Jesus better. The Holy Spirit teaches us and helps us to live as followers of Jesus.

How does water help you to remember what happens at Baptism?

TOGETHER AS A FAMILY

Share responses to the question on this page. After Mass visit the baptismal font or baptismal pool in your parish church. Bless yourself with water to remember that you are baptized.

Our Confirmation

WHAT WE SEE AND HEAR

Chrism is one of the three blessed oils used in the celebration of the sacraments. The other two blessed oils are the Oil of the Sick and the Oil of Catechumens. The place in the church where the blessed oils are kept is called the ambry.

The sacrament of Confirmation is the second Sacrament of Initiation. Confirmation strengthens our Baptism. Like Baptism, Confirmation marks us forever as a follower of Christ.

We are sealed with the Gift of the Holy Spirit. We receive the grace to live our Baptism. We may receive Confirmation only one time.

At Confirmation the bishop prays that God will bless all those to be confirmed with the Gift of the Holy Spirit. He prays that the Holy Spirit will help and guide us to live as children of God and followers of Jesus.

We come to the bishop with our sponsor. The bishop places his hand on our head. He greets us by name. As he anoints our forehead with chrism he says,

"Be sealed with the Gift of the Holy Spirit."

We respond, "Amen."

The bishop then says,

"Peace be with you."

We respond, "And also with you."

The sacrament of the Eucharist is the third Sacrament of Initiation. It joins us most fully with Jesus, the Son of God, and with all the members of the Church. It strengthens us to live as sons and daughters of God.

What happens at Confirmation?

TOGETHER AS A FAMILY

Share responses to the question on this page. This week talk about what it means to belong to the Church. Take time to pray the Apostles' Creed as a family. The Apostles' Creed is found on page 72 of this book.

What Difference Does This Make in My Life?

The Church is made up of the followers of Jesus. We are made followers of Jesus through the Sacraments of Initiation.

MY FAITH CHOICE

Talk with someone about one thing you will do this week to live as a follower of Jesus.

Draw a picture or write a story about how you can live as a follower of Jesus.

TOGETHER AS A FAMILY

Remembering Together

In this chapter your child learned about Baptism and the difference that being baptized makes in our lives. This is a good time for your family to share stories about family baptisms. Share any mementos with your child. Tell your child all about the day of his or her Baptism! Include:

- the reasons you chose your child's baptismal name
- the date and the name of the church
- the names of the godparents
- the name of the priest or deacon
- the names of the other people who celebrated with your family

Sharing Together

Choose one of these activities to do together or design a similar activity of your own:

- Have family members choose one thing they can do to live as followers of Jesus at home this week. Write and display the list to remind everyone of their choice.
- Make thank-you cards for your child's godparents or someone else who has helped your child grow in faith. Thank them for helping your child grow up as a follower of Jesus.

 Visit the RCL sacraments web site by following the link titled "Sacraments" at www.FaithFirst.com.

Praying Together

Pray this or a similar prayer at family meals or at other family prayer times this week:

God, our loving Father,
through the waters of Baptism
we become followers of Jesus Christ
and members of your Church.
Send us the Holy Spirit
to help us learn to live as your children.
We ask this in the name of Jesus Christ our Lord.
Amen.

Getting Ready Together

At the beginning of Mass, we bless ourselves by praying the Sign of the Cross. We remember our Baptism. We profess our belief in the Holy Trinity. We identify ourselves as followers of Christ.

This is an appropriate time to talk about and to practice praying the Sign of the Cross with your child. Praying the Sign of the Cross with meaning will help your child participate in the celebration of Mass.

CHAPTER 2

We Gather

Father, Son, and Holy Spirit, thank you for our church family.

Sharing Together

In the opening prayer we made the sign of the cross. We gathered together and walked in procession behind the cross. What was it like for you when you were following the cross?

Where do you gather with people?

The cross is a wonderful sign of Jesus' love for us. Give one example of a place where you see the cross.

I have seen the cross in the church, chruch, home, semetary, rosery necklace, the golden box. I the car.

The First Christians

Christians are followers of Jesus. The first Christians often gathered in one another's homes. Read this Bible story to discover why the first Christians gathered in one another's homes.

Many people were baptized and became followers of Jesus. They shared their food and everything they had. They helped one another live as Jesus taught them.

They spent time together learning about Jesus and praying together. They broke and shared bread with one another as the disciples did with Jesus.

BASED ON ACTS OF THE APOSTLES 2:41–47

FAITH FOCUS

Why did the first Christians gather in one another's homes?

The first Christians gathered together. When do you gather with your church family?

TOGETHER AS A FAMILY

Share the Bible story of the gathering of the first Christians. Then discuss responses to the question on this page. Explain that the first followers of Jesus had no churches to go to. Talk about why your family gathers at church each Sunday with other families who belong to your parish.

Our Church Family

WHAT WE SEE AND HEAR

The people who gather for Mass are called the assembly. The priest who leads the assembly in celebrating Mass is called the presider. The priest wears special clothes called vestments. The color of the vestments reminds us of the season or feast of the church year.

We gather as a church family. Our church family is the community of people who belong to Jesus Christ, the Son of God. The Church is the Body of Christ and the People of God. It is made up of people all over the world. Our church family also includes all the faithful members who have died.

Each Saturday evening and Sunday our church family comes together for Mass. The Mass is the most important celebration of our church family. At Mass we do what the first Christians did. We listen to God's word. We break bread. We receive Holy Communion. At the end of Mass we are sent out to live as followers of Jesus.

The priest leads our church family in the celebration of Mass. The Mass begins as the priest and other people walk in procession into the church. Everyone stands and sings a hymn. We remember that we all belong to our church family.

The priest greets us, saying, "The Lord be with you." We respond, "And also with you." We believe that God the Father, Jesus, and the Holy Spirit are present with us.

At Mass we worship God. We give adoration and honor to God. Together with Jesus we thank God the Father for his mercy. We praise God for his love. We ask God to help us live as his children. We are now ready to listen to the word of God.

Why do we gather for Mass?

TOGETHER AS A FAMILY

Share responses to the question on this page. Remind your child that God is present with your family, right in your home. Use the words "The Lord is with you. And also with you" to begin family prayers and family discussions. Use "Celebrating the Mass" on pages 62 and 63 of this book to help your child learn the responses for the introductory rites of the Mass.

What Difference Does This Make in My Life?

Each week on Sunday our church family gathers for Mass. We begin by signing ourselves with the sign of the cross.

MY FAITH CHOICE

Talk with someone about one thing you will do this week that shows you belong to our church family.

Circle the names of the people you see at Mass.

priest
reader
altar server
choir
deacon
church family
song leader

Draw a picture of yourself and of the other people you see at Mass.

TOGETHER AS A FAMILY

Remembering Together

In this chapter your child learned about the first Christians. They gathered in their homes. They shared all things in common. They prayed together and cared for one another. This is a good time for you to talk with your child about your own parish community. Review with your child the names of:

- your church or parish community
- your pastor
- other special people you know at church

Sharing Together

Choose one of the following activities to do together or design a similar activity of your own:

- The first followers of Jesus shared their food and other possessions with one another. Find out how your family can donate to a local food collection or shelter or parish service group that serves people in need.
- Find your family's photo albums. Look at the pictures and point out photos that show people following Jesus.

- Talk about ways your family can join in welcoming new members into your parish community. Then choose one thing that you will do together.

Visit the RCL sacraments web site by following the link titled "Sacraments" at www.FaithFirst.com.

Praying Together

Pray this or a similar prayer at family meals or at other family prayer times this week:

Loving God, our Father,
today we gather together in honor
    of your Son, Jesus Christ.
Send us the Holy Spirit
to help us remember to follow Jesus every day.
We ask this through Jesus Christ our Lord.
Amen.

Getting Ready Together

Use pages 62 and 63 of this book to go through the introductory rites of the Mass with your child. Review with your child the assembly's responses. This will help your child participate more actively and more fully in the celebration of Mass.

CHAPTER 3

We Listen

Good and loving God,
help us to listen to you.

Sharing Together

In the opening prayer we listened to a Bible story and we showed reverence for the Bible. We marked our forehead, lips, and heart with the sign of the cross. What was it like for you when you were signing yourself?

When do you read or listen to stories?

As Catholics we listen to and read the Bible. Give one example of a story from the Bible that you like to hear.

Adam and eve and When Jesus died on the cross.

Samuel Listens to God

The Bible has many stories about people listening to God. Read this story about Samuel. When Samuel was a young boy, his mother, Hannah, brought him to a priest named Eli. Eli taught Samuel about God.

One night Samuel was getting ready for bed. He heard a voice calling him. He thought it was Eli. So Samuel called to Eli, "Here I am." Eli called back, "I did not call you. Go back to sleep." Samuel went back to sleep. Two more times Samuel heard someone call his name. Each time he ran to Eli, saying, "Here I am."

Eli now knew it was God calling Samuel. So Eli said to Samuel, "The Lord is calling you. If the Lord calls you again, listen to him." Samuel went back to sleep. Again God called out, "Samuel, Samuel!" Samuel answered, "Speak, Lord, I am listening."

BASED ON 1 SAMUEL 3:1–10

FAITH FOCUS

What did Samuel do when he heard God's word?

Eli helped Samuel listen to God's word. Who helps you listen to the word of God?

TOGETHER AS A FAMILY

Share the Bible story about Samuel. Then discuss responses to the question on this page. Each day this week, choose a Bible story to read together. Before you begin, say together, "Speak, Lord, we are listening."

We Listen 25

The Liturgy of the Word

What happens at the Liturgy of the Word?

WHAT WE SEE AND HEAR

The Scriptures are read from a special place called the ambo. The first reading and second reading are read by the reader. After the first reading, we sing a psalm response. The Gospel is read by the deacon or priest. The first and second readings are read from a book called the Lectionary. The Gospel is read from the Book of the Gospels.

God speaks to us through the Bible. God gave us the gift of the Bible because he loves us. The Bible is also called the Sacred Scriptures. The word *sacred* means "holy." The word *scriptures* means "writings." The Sacred Scriptures are the written word of God.

The Bible has two parts. The parts of the Bible are the Old Testament and the New Testament. The Old Testament tells the story of God's people who lived before Jesus was born. The New Testament tells about Jesus and the first Christians.

Every Sunday at Mass we listen to three readings from the Bible. This takes place during the Liturgy of the Word. The Liturgy of the Word is the first main part of the Mass.

The first reading is usually from the Old Testament. It tells the story of God's love for us before Jesus was born.

The second reading tells us what the apostles and first Christians believed about Jesus. The apostles were the disciples Jesus chose to be the first leaders of his followers.

The third reading is the gospel reading. The word *gospel* means "good news." The four Gospels are part of the New Testament. They tell us who Jesus is and what Jesus did. Jesus shows us more than anyone else how much God loves us.

Why do we listen carefully to the readings during the Liturgy of the Word?

TOGETHER AS A FAMILY

Share responses to the question on this page with your child. Use pages 64 and 65 of this book to help your child learn the responses for the Liturgy of the Word.

What Difference Does This Make in My Life?

The Bible is God's word to us. We show reverence for the Bible because we believe it is God's word. When we listen to the Bible, we hear that God loves us.

Make a poster that tells others about the Bible. Use your poster as a reminder to listen with reverence to the word of God.

MY FAITH CHOICE

Read or listen to a gospel story with someone this week. Talk about what you learned about being a follower of Jesus.

Bible

TOGETHER AS A FAMILY

Remembering Together

In this chapter your child learned that the Bible is the written word of God. This is a good time for you to talk with your child about the Bible. Help your child come to know and reverence God's word:

- Take some time to look at the Bible and page through it with your child.
- Ask your child what is his or her favorite story in the Bible. Talk about what your child likes about that story and why it is his or her favorite story. Find that story in the Bible and read it together.
- Discuss what God's word to us might be in that Bible story.

Sharing Together

Choose one of the following activities to do together or design a similar activity of your own:

- In the early Church the followers of Jesus told each other about Jesus. Take time this week to tell your child about Jesus.
- Share an illustrated children's version of the Bible with your child. Invite your child to choose a gospel story. Ask him or her to read or tell the story to you, using the illustrations.

- Talk about how and why your church family listens attentively to God's word at Mass.

 Visit the RCL sacraments web site by following the link titled "Sacraments" at www.FaithFirst.com.

Praying Together

Pray this or a similar prayer at family meals or at other family prayer times this week:

Loving God, our Father,
you tell us about your love for us through the Bible.
Send us the Holy Spirit to help us grow in that love.
We ask this through Jesus Christ our Lord.
Amen.

Getting Ready Together

Use pages 64 and 65 of this book to go through the Liturgy of the Word with your child. Review with your child the assembly's responses. This will help your child participate more actively and more fully in the celebration of Mass.

We Give Thanks

*God of all creation,
thank you for
your blessings.*

Sharing Together

In the opening prayer we shared a variety of different breads with one another. What was it like for you when you were sharing the bread?

What can you share with others?

All our gifts are blessings from God. Sharing our gifts with other people is one way to say thank you to God. Give one example of a time when you shared with someone or someone shared with you.

_____

_____

_____

Jesus Feeds the People

The Bible tells us many stories about Jesus sharing bread with people. Read this gospel story. Discover how Jesus shows people God's love and care for them.

One day about five thousand people were listening to Jesus. That evening his disciples said, "Send the people away. They need to find a place to sleep and eat." Jesus said, "Give them something to eat yourselves." The disciples answered, "We have only five loaves of bread and two fish."

Jesus said, "Tell the people to sit down." Jesus then took the bread and fish. He looked up to heaven and blessed the food. He broke the bread into pieces. He gave the bread and fish to his disciples to give to the people.

Everyone ate until they were full.

BASED ON LUKE 9:10–17

FAITH FOCUS

How did Jesus show the people God's love for them?

Jesus fed the people to show God's love for them. When do you show people God's love for them?

TOGETHER AS A FAMILY

Share the Bible story about Jesus feeding five thousand people. For example: Talk about the illustration with your child. Have your child read the story to you. Or read a different version of the story from a children's Bible. Share responses to the question on this page.

We Give Thanks 33

The Liturgy of the Eucharist

FAITH FOCUS

What happens at the Liturgy of the Eucharist?

WHAT WE SEE AND HEAR

At Mass we always use bread and wine as Jesus did at the Last Supper. Wheat is used to make the bread, and grapes are used to make the wine. These become the Body and Blood of Jesus. The bread is unleavened bread. Unleavened bread is made without yeast.

God created everything and everyone out of love. God's love is so wonderful that he gave us the gift of his only Son, Jesus. Jesus showed us God's love. God's love for us lasts forever.

At Mass we thank God for all his gifts and blessings. We do this during the Liturgy of the Eucharist. The Liturgy of the Eucharist is the second main part of the Mass.

The word *eucharist* means "to give thanks." The Eucharist is one of the seven sacraments of the Church. It is the sacrament in which we receive Jesus, the Bread of Life, in Holy Communion.

We begin the Liturgy of the Eucharist by singing a hymn. As we are singing, some members of our church family carry our gifts of bread and wine in procession to the altar. The priest takes our gifts of bread and wine and prays two blessing prayers. Blessing prayers tell God we believe that everything we have comes from him.

The priest invites us to give thanks to God. We stand and pray:

Priest: Let us give thanks to the Lord our God.

Response: It is right to give him thanks and praise.

Together we sing to God. We sing, "Holy, holy, holy Lord."

Why do we thank God during the Liturgy of the Eucharist?

TOGETHER AS A FAMILY

Share responses to the question on this page. This week pray a blessing prayer at family meals. For example: Model your prayer on the blessing prayers at the beginning of the Liturgy of the Eucharist. Also use pages 66 and 67 in this book to help your child learn the Mass responses for the preparation of the altar and gifts and the preface.

What Difference Does This Make in My Life?

MY FAITH CHOICE

Talk with someone about one thing that you will do this week to show God you are thankful for the gifts he has given you.

All our gifts are blessings from God. The greatest gift God the Father gives us is his Son, Jesus Christ. At the celebration of the Eucharist we thank God for all his gifts to us.

Think about all the wonderful gifts God has given us. Draw or write about one gift that you want to thank God for.

Prayer of Thanksgiving

Thank you, God, for

All our gifts come from you. Amen.

TOGETHER AS A FAMILY

Remembering Together

In this chapter your child learned that it is important for us to give thanks to God. Use these or similar questions to talk together about how your family gives thanks to God:

- How do we give thanks to God for all creation?
- How do we give thanks to God for Jesus?
- How do we give thanks to God for people?
- How do we give thanks to God for our family?

Sharing Together

Choose one of the following activities to do together or design a similar activity of your own:

- Jesus fed about five thousand people to show them that God loves and cares for people. Find out how your family can donate to a local food collection.
- Invite a guest to share a meal with your family. As you plan, talk about how your family can share God's love with your guest.
- Sharing is one way we show God that we are thankful. Name the things that your family shares with one another.

 Visit the RCL sacraments web site by following the link titled "Sacraments" at www.FaithFirst.com.

Praying Together

Pray this or a similar prayer at family meals or at other family prayer times this week:

Loving God, our Father,
today we gather to celebrate the love
you share with each of us.
We give you thanks for all your gifts to us.
Send us the Holy Spirit
to help us remember to give you thanks every day.
We ask this through Christ our Lord.
Amen.

Getting Ready Together

Use pages 66 and 67 of this book to go through the preparation of the altar and gifts and the preface at Mass with your child. Review with your child the assembly's responses. This will help your child participate more actively and more fully in the celebration of Mass.

CHAPTER 5

We Remember

*Praise God for all
the wonderful things
he has done.*

Sharing Together

In the opening prayer we remembered what Jesus did for us. What was it like for you to pray this prayer?

What are some meals that help you to remember and celebrate something?

As Catholics we gather for Mass and share a meal to remember Jesus. Name one thing you remember about Jesus.

Jesuses birthday is on christmas,The baptisum of Jesus.

The Last Supper

On the night before Jesus died, he shared a Passover meal with his disciples. We call this meal the Last Supper. Read this gospel story. Discover what Jesus said and did at the Last Supper.

At supper Jesus took bread in his hands. He gave thanks to God. Then he broke the bread into pieces. He gave the bread to his disciples. Jesus said, "This is my body."

Next Jesus took a cup of wine. He gave thanks to God. Then he passed the cup to his disciples. Jesus said, "This is my blood. It is poured out for you for the forgiveness of sins."

Jesus told his followers, "Do this in memory of me."

BASED ON LUKE 22:17–20

FAITH FOCUS

What did Jesus say and do at the Last Supper?

Jesus celebrated the Last Supper with his disciples. When do we do what Jesus did at the Last Supper?

TOGETHER AS A FAMILY

Share the Bible story about the Last Supper. Then discuss the answer to the question on this page. Before each meal this week, thank God for bringing your family together to share the meal. Being together is what makes the meal special.

The Eucharistic Prayer

FAITH FOCUS

What happens during the eucharistic prayer?

WHAT WE SEE AND HEAR

Our church family gathers around the altar to celebrate our eucharistic meal. The altar is also called the table of the Lord. At the altar the bread and wine become our spiritual food. From the table of the Lord, we are fed with the Body and Blood of Christ.

At Mass the Church prays the eucharistic prayer. This prayer is the Church's great prayer of thanksgiving. During the eucharistic prayer we do what Jesus asked us to do at the Last Supper.

We call the Eucharist the Lord's Supper. At the Eucharist Jesus acts through the ministry, or work, of the priest. The priest does two important things during the eucharistic prayer. First, he asks God to send down the Holy Spirit. Second, he tells again the story of the Last Supper. The priest repeats the very words of Jesus. We call these the words of consecration. Through the power of the Holy Spirit the bread and wine become the Body and Blood of Christ.

The Eucharist is a holy sacrifice. It makes present the sacrifice of Jesus. Jesus sacrificed, or freely offered, his life on the cross to save us from our sins. At the Eucharist it is Jesus acting through the ministry of the priest who offers the eucharistic sacrifice. We offer ourselves to God the Father together with Jesus. We share in the death and resurrection of Jesus by the power of the Holy Spirit.

The Eucharist is also a promise. It is God's promise that all people who truly love God will one day live in heaven.

At the Eucharist we pray to God the Father through Jesus Christ together with the Holy Spirit. We remember and share in all Jesus did. We remember and share in his death and resurrection.

Why do we call the Eucharist the Lord's Supper?

TOGETHER AS A FAMILY

Share responses to the question on this page. This week talk about the ways that your family helps one another. For example: Talk about ways you care for one another when a family member is sick. Name ways that family members help one another with chores. Point out that when we do these things we are giving ourselves to one another out of love. We are learning what it means to make sacrifices.

What Difference Does This Make in My Life?

MY FAITH CHOICE

Talk with someone about one thing you can do this week to show that Jesus is always with us.

At Mass we remember and celebrate what Jesus said and did at the Last Supper. The bread and wine become the Body and Blood of Christ.

Color and decorate the picture. Remember that Jesus is with us in a special way at Mass.

TOGETHER AS A FAMILY

Remembering Together

In this chapter your child learned about the Last Supper and the eucharistic prayer. At Mass we remember and celebrate what Jesus did for us. Ask these or similar questions:

- What does our family remember and celebrate?
- How does our family remember Jesus?

Sharing Together

Choose one of the following activities to do together or design a similar activity of your own:

- Go to where the tabernacle is in your church. Pray together to thank God for the gift of Jesus, the Bread of Life.
- At the beginning of your next family meal, share stories about God's goodness.
- As a family, volunteer to bring up the gifts at Mass.
- If you do not have a symbol of Jesus in your home, make or display one to help your family remember Jesus.

 Visit the RCL sacraments web site by following the link titled "Sacraments" at www.FaithFirst.com.

Praying Together

Pray this or a similar prayer at family meals or at other family prayer times this week:

> Loving God, our Father,
> today we gather to remember your Son, Jesus Christ.
> We celebrate that Jesus is with us.
> Send us the Holy Spirit
> to help us live as Jesus did.
> We ask this through Christ our Lord.
> Amen.

Getting Ready Together

Use pages 67 and 68 of this book to go through the eucharistic prayer of the Mass with your child. Review with your child the assembly's responses. This will help your child participate more actively and more fully in the celebration of Mass.

CHAPTER 6

We Celebrate

Loving God,
thank you for giving us
Jesus, your Son.

Sharing Together

In the opening prayer we shared a sign of peace. We showed we believe Jesus is with us. What was it like for you when you shared a sign of Christ's peace?

When do you share peace with others?

The Easter candle also reminds us that Jesus is with us. Give one example of how you know Jesus is always with us.

I remember when I go to church or when I am sad.

The Road to Emmaus

After Jesus died on the cross, he was raised from the dead. Then Jesus appeared to his disciples. Read this Scripture story to discover what happened.

It was three days after Jesus died on the cross. Two of the disciples were going to a town called Emmaus. They talked about Jesus as they walked along the road.

Jesus came near the disciples. He began to talk with them. The disciples did not know that Jesus had been raised from the dead. They did not recognize him.

They arrived in Emmaus and the disciples invited Jesus to stay with them. They sat down to eat. Then Jesus took the bread in his hands. He blessed the bread. He broke it and gave it to the disciples. Then they knew he was Jesus. They recognized Jesus when he broke the bread.

BASED ON LUKE 24:13–35

FAITH FOCUS

What did the Risen Jesus share with his disciples?

The disciples recognized Jesus when he shared a meal with them. When do you know Jesus is with you?

TOGETHER AS A FAMILY

This week share this Scripture story with your child in different ways. For example: Invite your child to read to you the version on page 48 or a version from a children's Bible. Role-play the story as a family. Illustrate the story together, using paints, colored markers, crayons, or some other medium. Share possible responses to the question on this page.

Holy Communion

WHAT WE SEE AND HEAR

At Mass, after everyone has received the Eucharist, the leftover consecrated bread is placed inside the tabernacle. The consecrated bread is called the Blessed Sacrament. It is reserved there for those who are sick and for the devotion of the faithful.

The Risen Jesus is present with us at Mass. He shares with us the gift of his Body and Blood. At Mass we receive the gift of the Body and Blood of Christ in Holy Communion. Sharing Holy Communion joins us more closely with Jesus Christ and with all the members of the Church. We are made one with Jesus and with one another.

Jesus is the Bread of Life. In Holy Communion we are fed with the Bread of Life. We receive the strength to live as followers of Jesus and children of God. We receive the promise that we will live forever in heaven with God, Jesus, Mary, and all the saints.

We prepare our minds and hearts to receive Holy Communion. We stand and pray the Our Father. We remember we are one family. We are God's people. We share a sign of peace.

The priest breaks the consecrated bread that will be shared. We walk in procession to receive Holy Communion at the table of the Lord. The consecrated bread is the Body of Jesus. The consecrated bread is offered to us with the words, "The body of Christ." We respond, "Amen." We receive and eat the consecrated bread.

Next the cup of consecrated wine is offered to us with the words, "The blood of Christ." We respond, "Amen." Taking the cup in our hands, we drink the consecrated wine from the cup. The bread and wine we receive are the Body and Blood of Jesus.

TOGETHER AS A FAMILY

Share responses to the question on this page. This week proclaim your home as a dwelling of peace. For example: Create a small poster or plaque that reads "The Peace of Jesus to All Who Enter!" Display the poster near the entrance to your home. Also go over pages 69 and 70 to help your child learn the responses during the communion rite.

What happens when we receive Holy Communion?

What Difference Does This Make in My Life?

We receive the Body and Blood of Christ in Holy Communion. Our friendship with Jesus and with all the members of the Church is made stronger. We show that Jesus is with us when we live as peacemakers.

MY FAITH CHOICE

Talk with someone about one thing you will do this week to share the peace of Christ with others.

Use your own words to complete each sentence.

At Mass Jesus is with me when *I go up to the altar and see the Gold box.*

I can show Jesus is always with me when *I go to school. or when I pray when im good and help others.*

I live as a peacemaker when _____

Remembering Together

In this chapter your child learned about the Risen Jesus sharing a meal with the disciples. At the meal the disciples recognized Jesus when he broke the bread and shared it with them. At Mass we receive the gift of the Bread of Life. Jesus gives us the gift of himself. We share ourselves and Jesus with others in many ways. One way is to live as peacemakers. Use these or similar questions to help your child discover and live this important belief of our faith:

- How do we share peace with one another at church?
- How do we share peace with one another at home?
- How do we share peace with our neighbors?

Sharing Together

Choose one of the following activities to do together or design a similar activity of your own:

- Make a banner with the words *We Are All One in Jesus* on it. Display the banner where it can be seen by everyone in your family.
- At the beginning of your next family meal, share a sign of peace with one another.

- Brainstorm ways your family can be peacemakers with one another. Choose one thing that everyone will agree to do.

Visit the RCL sacraments web site by following the link titled "Sacraments" at www.FaithFirst.com.

Praying Together

Pray this or a similar prayer at family meals or at other family prayer times this week:

Loving God, our Father,
today you give us the gift
    of your Son, Jesus Christ.
Send us the Holy Spirit
to help us share the gift of Jesus
    by living as peacemakers.
We ask this through Jesus Christ our Lord.
Amen.

Getting Ready Together

Use pages 69 and 70 of this book to go through the communion rite of the Mass with your child. Review with your child the assembly's responses. This will help your child participate more actively and more fully in the celebration of Mass.

We Live

*Loving God,
thank you for the gift
of the Holy Spirit.*

Sharing Together

In the opening prayer we anointed our hands with oil. What was it like for you when your hands were anointed with oil?

When do you use oil?

As Catholics we often use oil in the celebration of the sacraments. Give one example of a sacrament that uses oil.

_____

_____

_____

The Gift of the Holy Spirit

Jesus sent the disciples, whom he chose to be the first leaders of the Church, to tell others about him. We call these disciples the apostles. Jesus promised that the Holy Spirit would come and help them. The Holy Spirit came to them fifty days after Jesus was raised from the dead. Read this Scripture story. Discover how the Holy Spirit came and helped the disciples.

On the day of Pentecost the disciples were gathered together in a house. Suddenly sounds of a loud, rushing wind filled the room. Small flames of fire settled above each of their heads. All of the disciples were filled with the Holy Spirit.

Next the disciples went out into the streets. The streets were filled with people. Peter told them all about Jesus. About three thousand people believed in Jesus and were baptized.

BASED ON ACTS OF THE APOSTLES 1:12, 2:1–42

FAITH FOCUS

What happened when the disciples received the gift of the Holy Spirit?

On Pentecost the Holy Spirit came to the disciples. When did you receive the gift of the Holy Spirit?

TOGETHER AS A FAMILY

Share the Bible story about Pentecost. Discuss responses to the question on this page. Before each family meal this week, thank God for the gift of the Holy Spirit. Name some of the ways your family can tell others about Jesus.

Live the Mass

FAITH FOCUS

At the end of Mass what are we sent forth to do?

WHAT WE SEE AND HEAR

At the end of Mass the priest extends his hands over us and asks God's blessing on us. The priest or deacon then sends us forth to live as disciples of Jesus.

At the Eucharist Jesus shares his divine life with us. He strengthens us to live as his disciples. We receive the grace of the Holy Spirit to live as Jesus taught us to live by what he said and did. He promised that the Holy Spirit would always be with the Church to help us.

The Bible tells us the Holy Spirit was always with Jesus. The Holy Spirit was with Jesus when he did his work on earth. Jesus told everyone how much God loved and cared for them. He healed people who were sick. Jesus forgave people's sins. He cared about people who were poor and told them how special they were to God. Everything Jesus said and did helps us come to know how much God loves us.

The Holy Spirit is with the Church today too. The Holy Spirit guides the Church to teach about Jesus and how to live as followers of Jesus.

At the end of Mass the priest asks God to bless us. We hear the words, "Go in peace to love and serve the Lord." We respond, "Thanks be to God." We thank God for making us disciples of Jesus. We share the gift of peace that God has given us.

Jesus told us that when we help people we are helping him. Filled with the Holy Spirit, we bring the good news of God's love to people. We tell others about Jesus. The Holy Spirit helps us to live as lights in the world.

What does it mean to be a disciple of Jesus?

TOGETHER AS A FAMILY

Share responses to the question on this page. Have each family member name one way your family can show it is a community of Jesus' disciples. Choose one suggestion and do it together. Use page 71 to review the Mass responses said during the concluding rite of the Mass with your child.

What Difference Does This Make in My Life?

The first disciples received the gift of the Holy Spirit on Pentecost. The Holy Spirit is with us too. The Holy Spirit is always with us as our helper and teacher.

MY FAITH CHOICE

Talk with someone about one thing you can do this week to show that the Holy Spirit is with you.

Write a prayer to the Holy Spirit to help you prepare for the Eucharist.

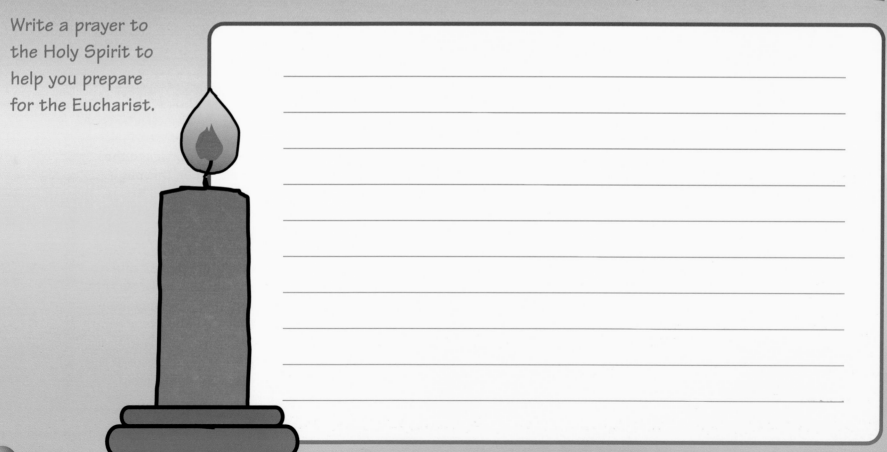

TOGETHER AS A FAMILY

Remembering Together

In this chapter your child learned that the Eucharist strengthens us to live as followers of Christ. At Pentecost the Holy Spirit came to the disciples and helped them tell others about Jesus. The Holy Spirit helps us live as Jesus' followers too. This week discuss with your child how your family can live as followers of Jesus. Use these or similar questions to guide your discussion:

- What are some ways our family continues the work of Jesus?
- How does our family show others that we live as followers of Jesus?
- How can we welcome the Holy Spirit into the life of our family?

Sharing Together

Choose one of the following activities to do together or design a similar activity of your own:

- Read John 14:15–31. Talk about how the Holy Spirit helps your family live as a Christian family.
- Write a prayer to the Holy Spirit. Pray the prayer together every day for a week.

- Name ways that your family can tell others about Jesus. Choose one thing you will do together as a family.

 Visit the RCL sacraments web site by following the link titled "Sacraments" at www.FaithFirst.com.

Praying Together

The Holy Spirit is our helper, teacher, and guide. This is an appropriate time to help your child learn this prayer. Make it a prayer your family prays each day as you begin the final preparation for your child to receive Communion.

Come, Holy Spirit, fill the hearts of your faithful.
And kindle in them the fire of your love.
Send forth your Spirit and they shall be created.
And you will renew the face of the earth. Amen.

Getting Ready Together

Use page 71 of this book to go through the concluding rite of the Mass with your child. Review with your child the assembly's responses. This will help your child participate more actively and more fully in the celebration of Mass.

Celebrating the Mass

Sunday is the main day for the celebration of the Eucharist. Sunday is the Lord's Day. It is the day of Jesus' resurrection.

INTRODUCTORY RITES

The Holy Spirit calls us to gather as the community of the Church. The Church is the People of God, the Body of Christ. We gather with Christ and one another. We prepare to listen to the word of God and to celebrate the Eucharist.

Entrance Procession and Gathering Song

We stand as the priest and other ministers enter the assembly. The priest presides over the celebration of the Mass. We sing a gathering song. The priest kisses the altar as a sign of reverence. The altar reminds us of Jesus and his love for us. The priest then goes to the chair where he leads us in praying the Sign of the Cross. We declare that Jesus is present with us.

Greeting

Priest: In the name of the Father, and of the Son, and of the Holy Spirit.

People: Amen.

Priest: The grace and peace of God our Father and the Lord Jesus Christ be with you.

People: And also with you.

Rite of Sprinkling with Holy Water

On some Sundays we are blessed with holy water to remind us of our baptism. We ask God the Father to help us be faithful to the Holy Spirit whom we have been given at Baptism. The Holy Spirit helps us live as children of God and followers of Jesus.

Penitential Rite

We admit our failures to live our baptism. We bless God for his mercy.

Priest: Lord, have mercy.

People: Lord, have mercy.

Priest: Christ, have mercy.

People: Christ, have mercy.

Priest: Lord, have mercy.

People: Lord, have mercy.

Gloria

On some Sundays we praise God the Father and Jesus, the Lamb of God, for the grace given us by the Holy Spirit. We celebrate that we share in the life of the Holy Trinity—God the Father, God the Son, and God the Holy Spirit.

Glory to God in the highest,
   and peace to his people on earth.
Lord God, heavenly King,
almighty God and Father,
   we worship you, we give you thanks,
   we praise you for your glory.
Lord Jesus Christ, only Son of the Father,
Lord God, Lamb of God,
you take away the sin of the world:
   have mercy on us;
you are seated at the right hand of the Father:
   receive our prayer.
For you alone are the Holy One,
you alone are the Lord,
you alone are the Most High,
   Jesus Christ,
   with the Holy Spirit,
   in the glory of God the Father. Amen.

Opening Prayer

We observe a moment of silence. We remember that we are in God's presence. We lift up our minds and hearts to God. We remember what God has done for us. We ask God the Father to help us live as children of God and followers of Jesus. The priest leads us in prayer.

Priest: Let us pray . . .

People: Amen.

Liturgy of the Word

The Liturgy of the Word is always celebrated at Mass. God speaks to us. We remember the story of God's love for us. Christ is present to us through his own word.

First Reading

We sit and listen as the reader reads from the Old Testament or from the Acts of the Apostles.

At the end of the reading the reader says:

Reader: The word of the Lord.

People: Thanks be to God.

Responsorial Psalm

The song leader leads us in singing a psalm. We make God's word our own.

Second Reading

The reader reads from the writings of the New Testament, but not from the four Gospels. At the end of the reading the reader says:

Reader: The word of the Lord.

People: Thanks be to God.

Alleluia or Gospel Acclamation

We show our reverence for Jesus, the Word of God. In Jesus, God most fully told us about himself and his love for us. We stand to honor Jesus present with us in the Gospel. The song leader leads us in singing "Alleluia." During Lent, we do not sing "Alleluia." We sing another Scripture verse.

Gospel

Priest
or deacon: The Lord be with you.

People: And also with you.

Priest
or deacon: A reading from the holy gospel according to (name of gospel writer).

People: Glory to you, Lord.

The priest or deacon proclaims the Gospel.

At the end of the Gospel, he says:

> **Priest**
> **or deacon:** The gospel of the Lord.
>
> **People:** Praise to you, Lord Jesus Christ.

The priest or deacon then kisses the Book of the Gospels.

Homily

The priest or deacon helps the whole community understand the word of God proclaimed to us. We choose ways to live as followers of Jesus.

Profession of Faith

We stand and profess our faith. Faith is accepting God's invitation to believe and trust in him. We pray the Nicene Creed or the Apostles' Creed (see page 72).

A creed is a prayer that tells what we believe. When we pray the Creed at Mass, we say that we believe in the Holy Trinity. The Holy Trinity is the belief that there is one God in three Persons: God the Father, God the Son, God the Holy Spirit. Each Person of the Trinity helps us live as children of God.

General Intercessions

The priest or deacon or another person leads us in praying for all people. We pray for the needs of the Church, for public authorities, for the salvation of the world, for people oppressed by any need, and for our local church community.

We can respond to each prayer in several ways. For example, after each prayer, we might respond:

> **People: Lord, hear our prayer.**

Liturgy of the Eucharist

Celebrating the Eucharist is the center of our Christian life. We join with Jesus through the power of the Holy Spirit to give thanks and praise to God the Father.

Preparation of the Altar and Gifts

The gifts of bread and wine are brought to the altar. The altar is the table of the Lord. We sit as the altar table is prepared and the collection is taken up. The song leader may lead us in singing a hymn.

The priest lifts up the bread and prays:

Priest: Blessed are you, Lord,
God of all creation.
Through your goodness we have
this bread to offer,
which earth has given and
human hands have made.
It will become for us
the bread of life.

People: Blessed be God for ever.

The priest lifts up the chalice, or cup, of wine and prays:

Priest: Blessed are you, Lord,
God of all creation.
Through your goodness we have
this wine to offer,
fruit of the vine and work
of human hands.
It will become our spiritual drink.

People: Blessed be God for ever.

The priest invites us to pray.

Priest: Pray, my brothers and sisters,
that our sacrifice
may be acceptable to God,
the almighty Father.

People: May the Lord accept the sacrifice
at your hands
for the praise and glory
of his name,
for our good,
and the good of all his Church.

Prayer over the Gifts

We stand and the priest leads us in praying the prayer over the gifts.

People: Amen.

EUCHARISTIC PRAYER

We pray the Church's great prayer of thanksgiving and sanctification.

The priest invites us to give praise and thanks to God the Father. We join in saying aloud or singing the **preface**.

Priest: The Lord be with you.

People: And also with you.

Priest: Lift up your hearts.

People: We lift them up to the Lord.

Priest: Let us give thanks to the Lord
our God.

People: It is right to give him thanks
and praise.

After the priest says or sings the preface, we join in saying aloud or singing the **acclamation**.

All: Holy, holy, holy Lord, God of power
and might,
heaven and earth are full of
your glory.
Hosanna in the highest.
Blessed is he who comes in the name
of the Lord.
Hosanna in the highest.

At the Last Supper Jesus gave us the Eucharist. The Eucharist makes Jesus' sacrifice of the cross present with the Church. At the Eucharist Jesus acts through the ministry, or work, of the priest. We recall what happened at the Last Supper. We share in the one sacrifice of Christ. The bread and wine become the Body and Blood of the Lord through the power of the Holy Spirit and the words of the priest. Jesus is truly and really present under the appearances of bread and wine.

After we do what Jesus asked us to do at the Last Supper in memory of him, we proclaim our faith in Jesus. We join in saying aloud or singing the **memorial acclamation**.

Priest
or deacon: Let us proclaim the mystery of faith:

People: Christ has died, Christ is risen, Christ will come again.

We remember Jesus' passion, death, resurrection, and ascension. The priest prays that God the Father accepts the Church's offering that we be filled with the Holy Spirit and become one with Christ. He then prays for the Church. He prays for the living and the dead and that we may one day live in heaven.

The priest leads us in proclaiming our praise of God by saying aloud or singing the **doxology** to conclude the eucharistic prayer.

Priest: Through him, with him, in him, in the unity of the Holy Spirit, all glory and honor is yours, almighty Father, for ever and ever.

People: Amen.

COMMUNION RITE

We prepare our minds and hearts to receive the Lord's Body and Blood.

Lord's Prayer

Jesus often told us about his love for his Father and his Father's love for us. In this prayer we call God "Father" as Jesus invited us to do. We tell God how much we love him and ask him for the grace we need to live as children of God. The Lord's Prayer is a summary of the Gospel.

Our Father, who art in heaven,
hallowed be thy name;
thy kingdom come;
thy will be done on earth as it is in heaven.
Give us this day our daily bread;
and forgive us our trespasses
as we forgive those who trespass against us;
and lead us not into temptation,
but deliver us from evil.

Priest: Deliver us, Lord, from every evil . . .

People: For the kingdom, the power
and the glory are yours,
now and for ever.

Sign of Peace

We prepare ourselves to receive the one bread and drink from the one cup. We share a sign of peace. We pray for peace and unity for the Church and the whole human family.

Priest: The peace of the Lord be with you always.

People: And also with you.

Priest
or deacon: Let us offer each other the sign of peace.

Breaking of the Bread

At the Last Supper Jesus broke bread and gave it to his disciples. At the time of the apostles the Eucharist became known as the "breaking of bread." The priest breaks the consecrated bread so it can be shared with others. Joining with him, we sing or say:

Lamb of God, you take away the sins of the world: have mercy on us.

Lamb of God, you take away the sins of the world: have mercy on us.

Lamb of God, you take away the sins of the world: grant us peace.

Communion

The priest drops a small piece of the consecrated bread into the consecrated wine. The priest raises the consecrated bread, or host, and proclaims that this is the Lamb of God. It is Jesus who takes away the sins of the world. We respond together by praying a prayer from the Gospel.

People: Lord, I am not worthy
to receive you,
but only say the word and
I shall be healed.

The priest receives Holy Communion. The faithful join in singing the communion hymn. We walk in procession to the altar to receive Holy Communion, the Body and Blood of Christ.

Priest: The body of Christ.

People: Amen.

We receive the consecrated bread in our hand or on our tongue. We reverently chew and swallow the consecrated bread.

If we are to receive the consecrated wine, the Blood of Christ, the minister offers us the cup.

Priest: The blood of Christ.

People: Amen.

We reverently take the cup in our hands and drink from the cup.

Period of Silence or Song of Praise

We return to our seats. We remember Jesus. We have received the gift of Jesus, the Bread of Life. We praise God for this wonderful gift.

Prayer after Communion

We stand as the priest invites us to pray. He prays that we are truly nourished and strengthened by our sharing in the Eucharist.

Priest: Let us pray.

People: Amen.

CONCLUDING RITE

Greeting

We stand. The priest greets us.

Priest: The Lord be with you.

People: And also with you.

Blessing

The priest blesses us in the name of the Holy Trinity. We remember that God loves us and shares his life and love with us now and for ever.

Priest
or deacon: Bow your heads and pray
                    for God's blessing.

Priest: May almighty God bless you,
                    the Father, and the Son,
                    and the Holy Spirit.

People: Amen.

Dismissal

The priest or deacon sends us forth to live the Great Commandment.

Priest
or deacon: Go in peace to love and
                    serve the Lord.

People: Thanks be to God.

The priest kisses the altar as a sign of reverence. He and the other ministers leave in procession. Everyone sings a hymn of praise.

Nicene Creed

We believe in one God,
the Father, the Almighty,
maker of heaven and earth,
of all that is seen and unseen.

We believe in one Lord, Jesus Christ,
the only Son of God,
eternally begotten of the Father,
God from God, Light from Light,
true God from true God,
begotten, not made, one in Being with the Father.
Through him all things were made.
For us men and for our salvation
he came down from heaven:
by the power of the Holy Spirit
he was born of the Virgin Mary, and became man.

For our sake he was crucified under
Pontius Pilate;
he suffered, died, and was buried.
On the third day he rose again
in fulfillment of the Scriptures;
he ascended into heaven
and is seated at the right hand of the Father.
He will come again in glory to judge
the living and the dead,
and his kingdom will have no end.

We believe in the Holy Spirit, the Lord,
the giver of life,
who proceeds from the Father and the Son.
With the Father and the Son he is
worshiped and glorified.
He has spoken through the Prophets.
We believe in one holy catholic and
apostolic Church.
We acknowledge one baptism for
the forgiveness of sins.
We look for the resurrection of the dead,
and the life of the world to come. Amen.

Apostles' Creed

I believe in God,
the Father almighty,
creator of heaven and earth.

I believe in Jesus Christ,
his only Son, our Lord.
He was conceived by the power of the Holy Spirit
and born of the Virgin Mary.
He suffered under Pontius Pilate,
was crucified, died, and was buried.
He descended to the dead.
On the third day he rose again.
He ascended into heaven,
and is seated at the right hand of the Father.
He will come again to judge the living and the dead.

I believe in the Holy Spirit,
the holy catholic Church,
the communion of saints,
the forgiveness of sins,
the resurrection of the body,
and the life everlasting. Amen.

Receiving the Eucharist

The Eucharist

Celebrating the Eucharist is the center of the life of the Church. The Catholic Church teaches that:

- The Eucharist is truly and really the Body and Blood of Christ.
- Only baptized Catholics may receive Holy Communion.
- Catholics are required to fast for one hour before receiving Holy Communion. This means that we are not permitted to eat food or drink anything, except for medicine and water.
- Catholics are encouraged to receive Holy Communion each time they go to Mass. Catholics are required to receive Holy Communion at least once a year during the Easter season. The Easter season begins at the Easter Vigil and ends on Pentecost Sunday.
- Catholics must be forgiven any mortal sins through the sacrament of Reconciliation before they receive Holy Communion.
- Receiving Holy Communion frees us from venial sins.

How to Receive Holy Communion

Follow these directions or the directions the teacher or catechist gives you:

- Walk in procession to the altar, singing the communion song, to receive Holy Communion from the priest, deacon, or eucharistic minister.
- You may receive Holy Communion either in your hand or on your tongue.
- The consecrated bread, or host, is offered to you with the words "The body of Christ." You respond, "Amen."

- If you choose to receive Holy Communion in your hand,
  — place one hand underneath the other hand,
  — hold your hand out with palms facing up, and
  — receive the consecrated bread in the palm of your hand.
  — Step to the side and briefly stop,
  — slowly and reverently take the consecrated bread from the palm of your hand, using the hand that is underneath the other, and put the consecrated bread in your mouth.
  — Chew and swallow the consecrated bread, the Body of Christ.
- If you choose to receive Holy Communion on your tongue,
  — fold your hands and open your mouth and put your tongue out to receive the consecrated bread.
  — Chew and swallow the consecrated bread.
- You may also receive the consecrated wine, the Blood of Christ. The cup of consecrated wine will be offered to you with the words "The blood of Christ." You respond, "Amen."
- If you choose to receive the Blood of Christ at Holy Communion,
  — take the cup of consecrated wine firmly in both hands,
  — using both hands, reverently bring the cup to your mouth,
  — take a small sip of the consecrated wine from the cup, and
  — carefully give the cup back, using both hands.
- Reverently return to your place, singing the communion hymn.
- Spend some time in quiet prayer and reflection after you have received Holy Communion.

My Daily Prayers

Sign of the Cross

In the name of the Father,
and of the Son,
and of the Holy Spirit.
Amen.

Glory Prayer

Glory to the Father,
    and to the Son,
    and to the Holy Spirit:
as it was in the beginning, is now,
    and will be for ever.
Amen.

Lord's Prayer

Our Father, who art in heaven,
hallowed be thy name;
thy kingdom come;
thy will be done on earth
    as it is in heaven.
Give us this day our daily bread;
and forgive us our trespasses
as we forgive those who trespass
    against us;
and lead us not into temptation,
but deliver us from evil.
Amen.

Hail Mary

Hail Mary, full of grace,
the Lord is with you!
Blessed are you among women,
and blessed is the fruit
    of your womb, Jesus.
Holy Mary, Mother of God,
pray for us sinners,
now and at the hour of our death.
Amen.

Grace before Meals

Bless us, O Lord,
and these your gifts
which we are about to receive
from your goodness.
Through Christ our Lord.
Amen.

Grace after Meals

We give you thanks for all your gifts,
almighty God,
living and reigning now and for ever.
Amen.

Morning Prayer

Dear God,
as I begin this day,
keep me in your love and care.
Help me to live as your child today.
Bless me, my family, and my friends
in all we do.
Keep us all close to you. Amen.

Evening Prayer

Dear God,
I thank you for today.
Keep me safe throughout the night.
Thank you for all the good I did today.
I am sorry for what I have chosen
to do wrong.
Bless my family and friends. Amen.

Glossary

A

altar

The altar is the table where the Liturgy of the Eucharist is celebrated at Mass. The altar is a sign of Christ's presence with us. It is also called the table of the Lord.

ambo

The ambo is a special stand or place from where the Scriptures are read at Mass.

anointing

Anointing is the signing of a person with holy oil. Anointing is used in the sacraments of Baptism and Confirmation, and in other sacraments and rites of the Church.

apostles

The apostles were the disciples Jesus chose to be the first leaders of his followers. Jesus sent the apostles forth to preach, to baptize, and to make disciples of all people.

Ascension

The Ascension is the return of Jesus to his Father in heaven to live with him in glory.

assembly

The people who gather to celebrate the Mass are called the assembly.

B

Baptism

Baptism is one of the Sacraments of Initiation. In Baptism we are joined to Christ. We share in Jesus' death and resurrection. God shares his life with us. We become adopted sons and daughters of God. We become members of the Church and followers of Jesus. Our sins are forgiven. We receive the Gift of the Holy Spirit.

Bible

The Bible is the written word of God. The Holy Spirit inspired, or guided, the people of God to write the Bible. The Old Testament and the New Testament are the two main parts of the Bible. The Bible is also called the Sacred Scriptures.

Blessed Sacrament

The Blessed Sacrament is a name given to the Eucharist, especially the Eucharist the Church keeps in the tabernacle for the sick and for the devotion of the people.

Book of the Gospels

The Book of the Gospels contains the gospel readings we listen to at Mass.

C

chalice

The chalice is the special cup used at Mass to hold the wine that becomes the Blood of Christ.

chrism

Chrism is oil blessed by the Church. The Church uses chrism in the celebration of the sacraments of Baptism, Confirmation, and Holy Orders and in other rites of the Church.

Church

The Church is the community of people who belong to Jesus Christ. The Church is the People of God, the Body of Christ, and the temple of the Holy Spirit.

Confirmation

Confirmation is one of the Sacraments of Initiation. In Confirmation the baptized celebrate and are sealed with the gift of the Holy Spirit.

consecration

The consecration is the rite of the Mass when we do and say what Jesus did at the Last Supper. The bread and wine become the Body and Blood of Christ by the words and actions of the priest and the power of the Holy Spirit.

creed

A creed is a prayer that tells what we believe.

D–E–F–G

disciple

A disciple is a person who learns from and follows the teachings of another person. At Baptism we become disciples of Jesus.

eucharist

The word *eucharist* means "give thanks."

Eucharist

The Eucharist is one of the Sacraments of Initiation. The Eucharist is the sacrament of the real presence of Jesus under the appearances of bread and wine. The Eucharist is the sacrament in which we receive the Body and Blood of Christ. The Eucharist makes present the sacrifice Jesus freely offered for the forgiveness of sins.

eucharistic prayer

The eucharistic prayer is the great prayer of thanksgiving that the Church offers to God the Father through Jesus Christ by the power of the Holy Spirit. We pray the eucharistic prayer at Mass.

Gospel

The Gospels are the first four books of the New Testament. The word *gospel* means "good news."

grace

The word *grace* means "gift." Grace is the gift of God's life and love the Holy Spirit shares with us. God's grace helps us to live as children of God and followers of Jesus.

H–I–J–K

Holy Communion

Holy Communion is receiving the Body and Blood of Jesus in the Eucharist.

Holy Spirit

The Holy Spirit is the third Person of the Holy Trinity.

Holy Trinity

Holy Trinity is a name for God. It tells us what God has told us about himself. There is one God in three Persons— God the Father, God the Son, and God the Holy Spirit.

host

The host is the name we give to the bread used at Mass.

hymn

A hymn is a song of joy, praise, and thanksgiving to God.

Jesus Christ

Jesus Christ is the Son of God, the second Person of the Holy Trinity, who became one of us. Jesus is true God and true man. By his death and resurrection Jesus saved us from our sins and reconciled us to God and to one another.

L

Last Supper

The Last Supper is the last meal that Jesus and his disciples shared together on the night before Jesus died on the cross.

Lectionary

The Lectionary is the book that contains the Bible readings proclaimed at Mass.

lector

The lector is the person who reads the first and second readings at Mass. Another name for lector is reader.

Liturgy of the Eucharist

The Liturgy of the Eucharist is the second main part of the Mass. In the Liturgy of the Eucharist we remember and share in Jesus' life, death, and resurrection.

Liturgy of the Word

The Liturgy of the Word is the first main part of the Mass. In the Liturgy of the Word God speaks to us through the readings from the Bible.

Lord's Supper

The Lord's Supper is another name for the Eucharist.

M–N–O

Mass

Mass is another name for the Eucharist. The Mass has two main parts: the Liturgy of the Word and the Liturgy of the Eucharist.

New Testament

The New Testament is the second part of the Bible. It tells us about Jesus and the early Church.

Old Testament

The Old Testament is the first part of the Bible. It tells the story of God's people who lived before Jesus was born.

P–Q–R

Paschal mystery

Paschal mystery is the name we give to Jesus' suffering, death, resurrection, and ascension.

Resurrection

The Resurrection is God's raising Jesus from the dead to new and glorious life by the power of the Holy Spirit.

reverence

Reverence is the gift of the Holy Spirit that enables us to show honor and respect to God, people, and all creation.

S–T–U

sacramentals

Sacramentals are objects and blessings that we use in worship and prayer. Sacramentals help us to remember that God is always with us. They help us to grow closer to God the Father, Jesus, and the Holy Spirit.

sacraments

The sacraments are the seven special celebrations of the Church that Jesus gave us. They are Baptism, Confirmation, Eucharist, Reconciliation, Anointing of the Sick, Holy Orders, and Matrimony. Jesus is present with the Church in a special way in the sacraments. Celebrating the sacraments makes us sharers in God's life and love.

Sacramentary

The Sacramentary is the book of prayers used by the Church for the celebration of Mass.

Sacraments of Initiation

The Sacraments of Initiation join us to Christ and welcome us into the church community. There are three Sacraments of Initiation. They are Baptism, Confirmation, and Eucharist.

Sacred Scriptures

The Sacred Scriptures are the written word of God. The Sacred Scriptures are also called the Bible.

sacrifice

A sacrifice is the giving of something important to God out of love. We share in the sacrifice of Christ at Mass.

sanctifying grace

Sanctifying grace is the gift of God's life and love. We receive sanctifying grace at Baptism. It makes us holy.

tabernacle

A tabernacle is a special place in which the Blessed Sacrament is kept.

V–W–X–Y–Z

vestments

The vestments are special clothes the priest wears to celebrate Mass and other sacraments.

worship

Worship means to give adoration and honor to God. At Mass we worship God. We join with Christ and the Holy Spirit to give thanks and praise to God the Father through our words and actions.

The Gift of the Holy Spirit

The Last Supper

The Road to Emmaus

Eucharist
Do this in memory of me.

"Do this
in memory
of me."

Based on Luke 22:19

All of the disciples
were filled
with the Holy Spirit.

Based on Acts of the Apostles 2:4

200 East Bethany Drive
Allen, TX 75002

They recognized
Jesus when
he broke the bread.

Based on Luke 24:31

T949